SHADOWS AND DAISIES

Sharon Webster

Tim Saunders Publications

TS
Tim Saunders Publications

Copyright © 2023 Sharon Webster

All rights reserved

No part of this book may be reproduced, or stored in a retrieval system, or transmitted in any form or by any means, electronic, mechanical, photocopying, recording, or otherwise, without express written permission of the publisher.

Cover design: Daisies by Kris Atomic

Richard, Robert, Matthew and Eleanor

Poetry is an echo that causes a shadow to dance

CARL SANDBURG

CONTENTS

Title Page	
Copyright	
Dedication	
Epigraph	
Introduction	
About	1
Ponderous Fleeting	2
Lascaux*	3
Legs sunk in loam have no ears	5
The softness of grey	6
City morning	7
Venice	8
Kandinsky*	9
It is not a trendy café	10
Luke's Grandma	12
The Vagrant of the Woods	13
People will ask	14
The reality of darkness	15
We gaze into tunnels	16
If you always walk on platforms	17

A journey of the mind	18
Dreams lose their colour without a sky	20
Too much water under the bridge	21
Moving on	22
We are sky gazers	23
Oh dear	24
A nod to the Impressionists	25
Sunset dreams	26
Forgetfulness	27
Autumn morning	28
School pick-up	29
Body balance	30
I am drowning in sheep	31
A world without borders	32
Stellar Forces	33
The Barn	34
The sky does not weep forever	35
Time for change	36
What colour is the sky?	37
The baggage that outlines us	38
The moon dance	40
The hole in the road	41
Afterword	42
Tim Saunders Publications	43

Photgraph: Kris Atomic

INTRODUCTION

If the order of these poems seems a little bit random, a little bit jumbled, then it is because life, I have discovered, is a little bit random, a little bit jumbled.

And if there seems to be a lot about the sky and nature and contemplating, more about good than bad, optimism and hope, instead of gloom and despair then you are right and perhaps a reflection of how I am lucky to see the world.

Sharon Webster

ABOUT

Sharon Webster lives in Cheltenham, Gloucestershire. She writes mainly poetry and short fiction inspired by the natural beauty she finds around her and the characters and lives of those who share her path. Sharon volunteers for Gloucestershire Writers' Network and has had success with her work in local anthologies and online.

PONDEROUS FLEETING

The sky is full of thoughts,
aging in the hush of the horizon,
layered in smouldering shades of dusk,
emotions unspoken,
unuttered truths.
Suspended there,
the dreams we have
dropped in rock pools,
or left imprinted in the
grass of languid shade,
hopes, unsullied in the sunrise,
then tarnished
by the mud
of thunder rain,
an essence,
a fragment of ourselves,
abandoned in those paths
brushed by our days.

LASCAUX*

"Can you see the movement?"

The young man edged his way to the front of the group that was standing expectantly in the cool darkness of the cave and inclined his head to follow the outline made by the guide's red light on the wall. There, softly illuminated, were the upper bodies of three reindeer. They were positioned, as if in a line, all facing the same direction and beautifully painted in tones of red and orange, yellow and black. In fact, the entire wall was covered in animal images but these three had been painted to be together, and the artist, without adding anything more, had somehow conveyed the impression that they were in water.

As the group moved on, he sank to the floor for a moment, overwhelmed. Yes, he had seen the movement. He had seen the ripples extending out widely as they made their way across the river, smelt the dust in their coats, heard the gentle lap as the waves ran up against the mossy banks. There was the sound of their hooves and the vibration as they thundered across the hard terrain and then there was the defiance in their bellow as it resonated across the valley.

Yes, he had seen the movement. He was just not sure how.

* Lascaux is a network of caves near the village of Montignac, in the Dordogne, France. Over 600 parietal wall paintings cover the interior walls and ceilings of the cave.

LEGS SUNK IN LOAM HAVE NO EARS

Legs sunk in loam
have no ears,
and arms abandoned in cardigans
cannot colour
the outside of homes,
tame butterflies
liberated from crushed
attic spaces,
or ride on chariots
hewn of the inky black.

THE SOFTNESS OF GREY

Sunrise,
the morning mist
a honeyed haze,
behind a storm weathered,
deep impression
made
in mud,
brambles broken
in the frantic rush of gloom,
and I am slipping, sliding,
pooling, puddling,
with this softness of grey,
along shrouded valley paths
into the new.

CITY MORNING

Day breaks across the city.
Its silhouette of spires
and domes and angles,
melts away in pools and
criss-cross lines of light.
Streets, bereft of sleep,
fill with trams and
cars and buses.
And parallel lives collide,
waiting in queues,
crossing on bridges.

Photograph: Nature's Beauty

VENICE

Light pools on silken
triangles and spheres,
drips like dew to
honeyed circles
that repeat, repeat,
and pristine chapels in
ancient squares
brim silently with reverence
and prayers are echoes,
footsteps, voices
dulled in
damp passages,
stone bridges,
the link
to eras past.

KANDINSKY*

If we stand in the rain,
drops will fall on our heads.
And if we linger in puddles,
our feet will get wet.
And some will have hats,
umbrellas and boots, and
for them the experience
will not be the same.

* Wassily Wassilyevich Kandinsky (1866 to 1944) was a Russian painter and art theorist. He is one of the pioneers of abstraction in western art, after Hilma af Klint. Born in Moscow, he spent his childhood in Odessa, where he graduated from Grekov Odessa Art School.

IT IS NOT A TRENDY CAFÉ

It is not a trendy café,
it is for old people
but they are not old
this couple who
command my attention.

They are having a row,
inevitable since her carefree arrival,
him strumming his foot,
bolt upright at the table,
his slamming his cup
quite fiercely down.

He is a Greek god but
she eclipses him
and I am not alone
in my observing,
in my wincing,
as the storm begins,
my gaping at
the fire,
the theatre of his departure.

She leans forward,
pushes dark curls
behind her ear,
slowly sips her now cold brew

and smiles.
"Wow," I mutter under my breath.
What's that?" my Greek god
replies from behind his newspaper.

LUKE'S GRANDMA

There were flowers in her hair, hair that
tumbled in rebellious waves
to her shoulders,
and hardened feet that
danced in the dew
across the grass.
And the grass, meadow long,
and the weeds tall for,
"They are not weeds if they are
pretty and people like them…"
Her hands picked fruit from trees
which was eaten without being wiped
and there were goats, and hens, and digging…
There was no phone, no telly, no car,
just walking, and reading, and singing.
Her choice,
it had always been so,
for she was not old at the beginning,
not losing it,
just free.

THE VAGRANT OF THE WOODS

A quarrel on a bright spring day,
and so, a solitary ramble.
Distracted,
I must have tripped,
or slipped,
or something,
for I tumbled,
rolled down and down
a mossy bank,
and weathered arms,
they caught me,
I looked up,
such a lonely face,
I knew no malice
was it seeking.
It was a moment,
a mystical exchange,
as if
the trees,
the breeze,
were speaking.

PEOPLE WILL ASK

People will ask,
"How was it for you,
the lockdown?"
And I will say,
"It was yellow and blue,
full of noisy silence
and the smell of
baking, paint and glue."
I will tell them,
we were all at home,
alone, together,
that families played,
that it was a different world,
sort of eerie,
sort of nice,
and that it lasted
days and days and days.

THE REALITY OF DARKNESS

Her darkness had been a lover,
a velvet touch, a dare, a game,
a giggle under soft covers.
The fury held in clouds of thunder rain.
Its chill, just a first plunge into the sea,
an unfair shoulder,
or winter waiting for the bus
and its silence a gift, a linger,
a savoured stillness
but now this.
A sinking into,
a spiralling grey abyss,
existence, a listening,
a fearful anticipation of a tread,
the clock hands turning on
choking, overwhelming,
drenching dread.
And she had thought herself so
brave, so strong,
the first to dive into the water,
the burning building,
a leader, a protester.
She had been wrong

WE GAZE INTO TUNNELS

We place our feet on eggshells
thin veneers,
forgetful of the filth
that floats in fiery eddies underneath.
And we speak
as if in vacuums,
tune into white noise,
gaze into tunnels.
So, of course, we are surprised
by the explosion,
the plume of smoke,
the burning ash,
the stench of devastation.

IF YOU ALWAYS WALK ON PLATFORMS

If you always walk
on platforms,
smooth,
raised above the ground,
how will you learn
where you might stumble?
And without a mist or fog
how can you see?
Eat only the fruit
of your garden and you
will only ever be a judge.
Never play the game,
and you will never
know how good
the game
can be.

A JOURNEY OF THE MIND

The picture is a lullaby, a pastel shade, a whispered voice. It is the touch of blossom casually brushing your face as it falls from the trees and the taste of honey, a giggle or the tinkle of a stream passing across moss splattered rocks. It is instantly uplifting but is, itself, confined, retained within the outline of a small rectangle. Placed in an insignificant portion of a much larger page, it will be imprinted on my mind forever whilst its neighbours barely skim my consciousness, before fading from my field of view.

I could compare the find to that of a book stumbled upon in a cluttered shop. It is the one you loved in childhood, read to your own offspring over tea, the epic you devoured yourself as a younger adult somehow, inexplicably forgotten. It is the well-leafed, jammied* friend, the truly favourite collection of pages. Seeing it again after such a time, and not quite in the same guise as that original copy, you might struggle a little with the details of the plot, the exact sequence of the story, but you will not struggle with the emotion, with how it made you feel. No, you will remember that.

There is no water in the picture yet I can hear it. I wade in in welly boots risking the spill over of the centre. I mess about on the banks adding my squeals to those of my young friends, hoarding my collections of rocks and vegetation. And then, as an older person, I wander, ponder close to the edge, taste the freshness of the spray, feel the cool green dampness of it. And I smile.

And there is no movement. Yet I can feel it, the gentle ripple of a breeze that lifts my hair from my forehead and cools my legs and though I cannot see any birds, their song embroiders the air everywhere.

The image cries out from the straight lines and monochrome that surround it and so I find the scissors and set it free.

Across the table some other person is examining the hustle and bustle of a street scene.

I return to my woodland and its carpet of blue.

* north-west slang for lucky

Photograph: Bob Richards

DREAMS LOSE THEIR COLOUR
WITHOUT A SKY

They took away the view, the sky,
subdued it behind a wall of brick and glass,
measured fences, solid screens,
so now the swirling blossom, the dancing leaves
are just foundations for houses.
And nothing is random or beautiful any more.
The colours, the dappled brightness,
shadows, silhouettes,
the fields and sheep and hedges,
still precious images
inside my head
but my dreams lack colour,
without the vastness of the blue,
the excess of the stars
the magic of the moon.
Wise men, what have they done?
This little brush with bliss
completely gone.

TOO MUCH WATER UNDER THE BRIDGE

I am an island off a rugged coast,
protected by a choppy sea,
and raging winds and rocky spurs,
rare plants, perhaps endangered birds.
My shores unsafe for strong foundations,
for bridges people have in mind,
amends for words, hurt, accusations,
things they've done that were unkind.
So grateful for this gulf between us,
I'm living freely, far remote...
Perhaps one day,
in calmer waters,
I may grant access
if in a boat.

MOVING ON

The squares sit together at the end of the drive, alongside the boxes, the perfect cubes. They are too many to count but neatly aligned, practical, tasteless, hateful. On the other side are bags, their contents protruding like hernias into the space between them, amorphous shapes that reach out to touch their neighbours and irregular pots coloured in the warm memories of our leisure. And there you are *on it* and here I am, flowing, flapping in and out.

WE ARE SKY GAZERS

We sit on coloured towels
and patterned rugs,
folding bits of wood,
and solid benches,
look out from
rounded hills,
brown, barren cliffs,
and wind-blown beaches.
We watch from margins,
scrutinise from edges.
Wizened questions,
they occupy our minds,
the whats, the wheres,
the whos, the whys.
And these age-old conundrums,
we lay them down,
place them gently
at the feet,
of this great union
of the earth and sky
impossibly expectant.
Yet here,
they come
….. answers.

OH DEAR

The cracks on the pavement,
they don't trip you up.
It is not the ice,
the dampness of the leaves,
the small dog on a thin lead.
It is not the child,
the old lady in a crowd,
the step,
the sudden stop.
Nor the noise,
the boisterous boys,
the guy late for his bus,
the funny story overheard,
it is not us.
You just trip up,
and then we trip up.

A NOD TO THE IMPRESSIONISTS

I want to see the world
as if from your eyes,
vibrant, colourful and bright,
the definition of your brushstrokes
disguising dullness
in soft light.
I want my world to be
the one that you saw,
filled with elegance and style,
friendship, talent,
culture, interest,
those I want to stay
a while.
The canvases, they tell a story,
a glimpse of what
you had,
and I envy you the beauty,
the everyday much richer,
the charm,
the nothing bad.

SUNSET DREAMS

In weightless dreams
I swirl and leap
entranced.
The echo of the sea,
its soulful melody,
the music to my dance
I plunge and dive
in shimmering fires of light;
loiter in the beauty of the night.
Charmed by ripples
racing in the breeze,
the flight of birds,
the motion,
the magic of this sunset,
in my sleep,
across the ocean.

FORGETFULNESS

There's no more space
inside my head,
no room for
routine contemplation,
can't guarantee
that lists or tasks,
or really anything
you ask,
with any speed
be undertaken.
I listen but
I might not hear.
Though present,
I am somewhere else,
I float about,
do not achieve
I smile and hum,
mid-sentence leave.
I'm not myself
but more than fine
warm thoughts of love
just fill my mind.

AUTUMN MORNING

I will run and gather up the light,
fill my arms with rosy morning haze.
Scoop some of the fiery evening spice,
the citrus blue crispness of the days.
I will take a morsel of the mist,
that swirls and pirouettes amongst the trees,
a slither of the stillness and the peace,
the muffled scrunch of boots,
the gentle drip of rain,
on fallen leaves.
I will need an imprint
of the vastness of the sky,
the silhouette of distant hills.
And I will keep them safely,
as a memory just in case
I can no longer spend my autumn
in the beauty of this place.

SCHOOL PICK-UP

The storm has passed,
dark clouds that gathered quickly,
rain that fell in torrents,
now all gone.
I am breathless,
drenched, beneath an apologetic sun.
In time,
despite the unexpected sprint,
the sudden dash,
to see her furtive peek
through classroom blinds,
her little smile,
delighted,
I pretend I've
been here for a while.
Bombarding me with all her news,
we trundle home,
a few large puddles
catch our eye.
Today, it seems,
there is no script,
it is not fun,
to do those things
that tend to keep us dry.

BODY BALANCE

I hear the rhythm,
feel the beat,
the vibration
from the ground.
I am already smiling,
swaying, moving.
primeval instincts
triggered
by the sound.
A warm up,
a focus on the breath.
The room's energy
building,
I follow the steps.
Then lost in the music
I hinge, lunge, dive.
My inner dance
found now
I'm truly alive...

I AM DROWNING IN SHEEP

I am drowning in sheep,
wave after wave,
pulsing over the hill.
I am crushed by the sheep,
their pushing and barging,
the noise, all that baaing,
and my head's in a spin
with the din,
as I toss and I turn,
elusive the sleep,
but still there is sheep,
nothing but sheep.

A WORLD WITHOUT BORDERS

The sun turns round,
trees weep flames
that swirl,
with splintering
rays of gold
to puddled ground.
And swallows,
silhouettes
against the
careless streaks
of blue on white,
rally with their cry,
in the exuberance of their dives
a call to flight.
And for a moment,
I am
grey and flat,
a rectangle,
an empty bowl.
For they will take with them
the summer,
and there will be a little sadness
in my soul.

STELLAR FORCES

My favourite
star has gone.
Seized by
shadows in
the darkness.
Drawn deep, deep,
down into oblivion.
A more pallid
breach perhaps
the portal
now
to fill
the space
with some,
as yet,
unrecognised,
alien
shimmer.

THE BARN

From the yard it was possible to see right through the old barn to the gentle curves of the valleys and hills beyond, the solid wood of the doors at either end framing the view. And you could stand right in the middle of it and still be bathed in light as the sun came up over the hill, warm golden rays that illuminated the rafters and threw the dust into a frenzy. At harvest time it was full of workers and chickens and children and even in the bad months it was a favourite place, to linger, have a chat, protected from the rain and the blizzards. It had always been so.

It was in the barn the man found himself, after the telegram. He stayed there in the reassuring solidity of that place, the only scrutiny that of the shires, their warm breath hanging in the autumn air, and held it close.

The world would go on. The farm would go on but not now with his boy. He would find the strength to cope.

He just hadn't found it yet.

THE SKY DOES NOT WEEP FOREVER

The sky is weeping,
coloured steely grey with dust,
indifferent to the sobbing,
the wailing, the tortured anguish
of the cold hopelessness,
and the ground is groaning,
bruised by the battering,
bewildered by the destruction,
the abruption of right,
and a man is searching,
outwardly deaf,
seemingly blind.
Yet in the rubble
a remnant, a fragment
of his ordinary life.
He holds it tight.
He holds on tight.
It is worth the fight.

And when the storm has passed,
brightness will seem more bright,
the peace much quieter,
the mundane a jewel,
more cherished than
otherwise, it might.

TIME FOR CHANGE

Today the sun will rise,
and we shall be shadows,
short and fat, lean and tall,
it will not matter.
There will be work and play,
eating and sleep, and love and hate,
and happiness and grief,
because there always is.
But it could be the day
the sun turns round,
the day the world begins
to spin another way,
the day a voice is heard,
"enough"
and shadows merge,
and make the
nonsense stop.
It's in our hands.

WHAT COLOUR IS THE SKY?

"What colour is the sky ?" you ask,
and I glance up,
reply "It's blue."
Then you include the fields and grass,
the forests, the tall mountain pass,
the oceans and the windswept dunes,
Their colours seemed important too.
You asked me
"Does the sun still rise?
Do other people wake and work,
and wash and eat,
and smile and laugh?"
I got it then,
how much you'd lost.

THE BAGGAGE THAT OUTLINES US

When she was a little girl she lived in the city.
There were no meadows there,
no daisy chains
but there were parks and
pockets of earth in
the corners of squares,
dusty allotments,
and garish pots on balconies
and in the posh bits
there were spaces,
gaps in gated railings,
glimpses of lawns with
formal flowerbeds
and ornamental trees,
perfect, frustrated.
It was not quite enough.

In the middle bit she lived
by the sea, a no-man's land
neither earth nor sand,
too salty, too windy,
nothing ever grew.
Expansive, wild, spirited and free,
she knew, she knew
she would have to leave one day,
but for a little while so was she.

SHADOWS AND DAISIES

In the twilight was a cottage,
a gravel path,
a tumbling randomness of colour
fragranced from the past.
The hedge though was cut in waves
and she drew illustrations on all her walls,
that were quite bonkers,
quite rebellious,
that's how she'd
come to see it all.
And this was enough.

Photograph: Travel Photographer

THE MOON DANCE

The moon splinters on the surface of the ocean,
its shards of light scattered to the
fringes of the night,
and at the reaches of the tides,
a silhouette of silver motion,
the steps a story of the earth,
of birth and death,
of fear and tenderness and life.
For in the silence of the stillness
can be heard a rhythmic beat,
born of the murmur
of the waves and winds and trees.
It is echoed in the pounding of bare feet,
in the exuberance of the swirling jumps,
the leaps.
The dance an age-old calling,
an expression of the bliss,
to be alone beneath the stars
on such a night as this.

THE HOLE IN THE ROAD

It was a large hole, the largest we in the village had ever seen and, appearing overnight as it did, right there in the middle of the road, it caused a lot of trouble, I can tell you.

Of course, there were theories, there would be in a village like ours. Some thought it had been made by a UFO landing or, at the very least a comet targeting the village from outer space. Others that Frank and his cronies had dug the hole on purpose to make a statement, reduce the traffic through the village, reduce the danger and the pollution sort of thing. And there were those who thought it was just the kids messing about, trying to divert the hedgehogs or the frogs from their habitual crossing.

Anyway, one day a man came from the council, stood right in the middle of the hole, he did, never said nothing to no-one just stood there looking out. Then he took a brush and made a circle right round the hole, bright yellow it was, could see it a mile off. Anyway, the next day the hole was gone, disappeared, even the yellow circle. Now we are all on the lookout. No one has spotted any more holes yet but Jack did have a tree fall down right across his drive, landed in the shape of an S it did. It was the strangest thing.

AFTERWORD

When she was a little girl my daughter wrote a poem and, with her permission, I share it with you here.

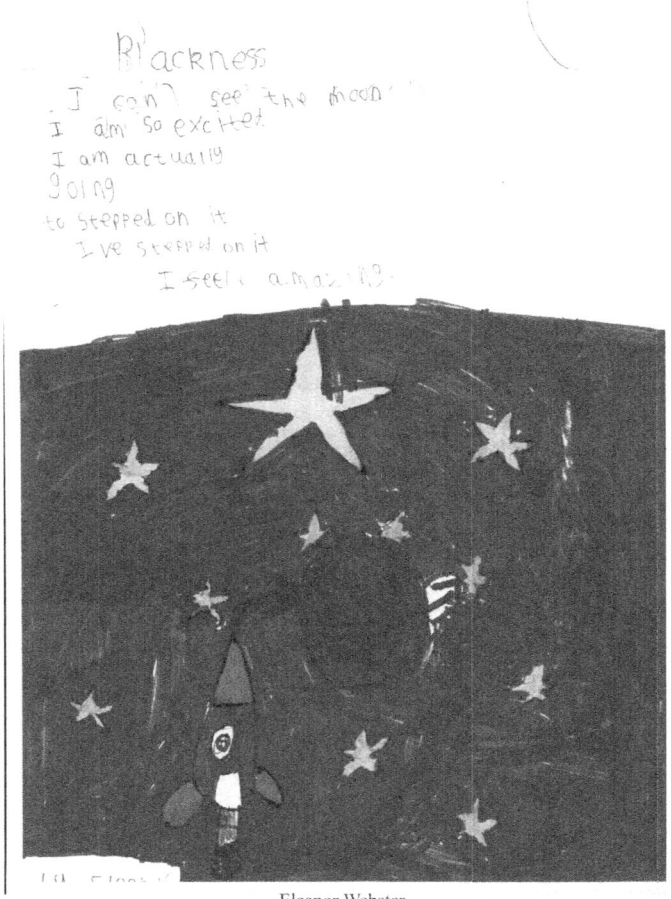

> Blackness
> I can't see the moon
> I am so excited
> I am actually
> going
> to stepped on it
> I've stepped on it
> I feel amazing

Eleanor Webster

TIM SAUNDERS PUBLICATIONS
art, poetry, fiction and memoir

"Everybody has a book in them," according to journalist Christopher Hitchens (1949 to 2011)

Do you have a book you would like to publish?

Email. tsaunderspubs@gmail.com

For more information visit:
tsaunderspubs.weebly.com

Unsolicited submissions welcome.

Printed in Great Britain
by Amazon